T0158888

Thank you Renee P. Aldrich for developing a symposium that really touched the heart of the reasons we stay stuck. The event was heartwarming, elegant, and supportive. Please continue to do the life changing work that God places on your hearts

Sandra Lee (Penn Hills) – attended 11/1/2014 & 2015 SSS WOMAN TO WOMAN EMPOWERMENT

Renee, this was a wonderful event and it was a pleasure being amongst many strong and inspiring women. I look forward to attending your next event. As you shared in your opening speech, I was also reminded of this: Deuteronomy 31:6 – "6 Be strong and courageous. Do not be afraid or terrified because of them, for the Lord your God goes with you; he will never leave you nor forsake you."....

JacQuelyne Huggins-Hill

This year's Woman to Woman Empowerment Symposium was filled with powerful positive electric energy. Personally my spirit was engaged, and I was able to identify hard truths. Renee's work brings about self-evaluation and soul searching—both of which are important to the pathway to self-love. The tools and lessons we gathered at the event are within the pages of this wonderful volume—it should be read, and shared between women and their daughters, their nieces, their granddaughters and any woman the love—a healthy spirit makes a healthy life—thus *Notes From the Softer Side*

In Art's Way—Eileen Morris, Artistic Director Ensemble Theater—Houston TX

Thanks Renee for inviting me to facilitate the panel of women –pulling themselves from the Stuck Places.. There is power in such a forum... Softer Side Seminars—a program whose time is come...

Erica Upshaw-Givner, Lead Clinician
—Vision Towards Peace Therapeutic Services

Notes
from the
Softer Side

A Roadmap to Achieving
God's Plan for Your Life

RENEE P. ALDRICH

BALBOA.
PRESS
A DIVISION OF HAY HOUSE

Scripture quotations marked NIV are taken from the Holy Bible, New
International Version®. NIV®. Copyright © 1973, 1978, 1984 by International
Bible Society. Used by permission of Zondervan. All rights reserved. [Biblica]

Balboa Press books may be ordered through booksellers or by contacting:

Balboa Press
A Division of Hay House
1663 Liberty Drive
Bloomington, IN 47403
www.balboapress.com
1 (877) 407-4847

Because of the dynamic nature of the Internet, any web addresses or
links contained in this book may have changed since publication and
may no longer be valid. The views expressed in this work are solely those
of the author and do not necessarily reflect the views of the publisher,
and the publisher hereby disclaims any responsibility for them.

The author of this book does not dispense medical advice or prescribe the use
of any technique as a form of treatment for physical, emotional, or medical
problems without the advice of a physician, either directly or indirectly. The
intent of the author is only to offer information of a general nature to help you
in your quest for emotional and spiritual well-being. In the event you use any
of the information in this book for yourself, which is your constitutional right,
the author and the publisher assume no responsibility for your actions.

Any people depicted in stock imagery provided by Thinkstock are models,
and such images are being used for illustrative purposes only.
Certain stock imagery © Thinkstock.

Print information available on the last page.

ISBN: 978-1-5043-7481-1 (sc)
ISBN: 978-1-5043-7483-5 (hc)
ISBN: 978-1-5043-7482-8 (e)

Library of Congress Control Number: 2017902386

Balboa Press rev. date: 08/12/2017

THIS WORK IS DEDICATED TO THE MEMORY OF

My Grandmother   Erin Godfrey—Entrepreneur

My Mother   Araminta Godfrey—stalwart leader

My Beloved Mom/Aunt   Erin Godfrey Mittchell
"Because she wrote—I write"

These Women whose strength, wisdom, fortitude, devotion to family and who stood uncompromised and unapologetically in a softer more loving place with themselves—before I even knew it was a "thing" to do or be. And therefore created a space for us to flourish, to stand the test of this life, to raise our children, and face life's trials starring them down—and though not perfect—continue daily striving to GET IT DONE...

THIS WORK IS DEDICATED TO THE MEMORY OF

What does this Mean?

That for too long we have been trapped in a cycle of guilt from past mistakes, low self esteem, and feelings of inadequacies. We believe the negative identifiers that others have used about us.

We don't believe that we can rise out of our situations, the main reason we don't believe we can, is because we have convinced ourselves that we do not deserve to be in a better place in life.

We allow ourselves to be abused by others, and we add to the abuse by placing the needs of others in our life above ours.

Through Softer Side Seminars we work to break those cycles and administer the charge to all women to answer the call to enter into a softer more loving relationship with ourselves and;

- Commit to trust, love, honor, and respect the beautiful gifted woman God made when He made you

- Commit to entering into a softer more loving relationship with ourselves—We will commit to Embracing the softer side

INTRODUCTION

"For I know the Plans I have for you declares the "Lord to Prosper you and not to harm you, Plans to give you hope and a future"
Jeremiah 29:11

In April of 2000 I was working as a community health educator with the Pittsburgh Office of the American Cancer Society and had been working there for a month when I was invited to the first of many luncheons and events. It was the African American Women's Speaker Bureau first annual prayer breakfast.

The AAWSB was a group of women of color interested in educating women about their risk for developing breast cancer. There was a full program including a morning speaker. She was the wife and co-pastor of a local non-denominational church. I recall vividly this woman had a title and referred to herself as Prophetess (we'll call her Mary Carter). I didn't particularly find that appealing and made a point that while I was going to support some of my colleagues, I definitely would be sure to stay out of the way of the "prophetess"—I wasn't particularly a proponent of being read by someone who could *read* the future—so I made a note to steer clear. However at the end of the morning, my good manners prevailed, and I approached the front of the room to thank the speaker.

She shook my hand as I engaged her in what was intended to be a cordial exchange, "thank you for that inspiring message", and then she might have said, "thank you my sister, God is good." Now, that did happened, but when we shook hands and she walked away, she abruptly turned back to me and said, "Wait, wait, I'm sensing a book in you; is there something you are waiting on?" After I picked my chin up off the floor, and was furtively seeking a way to a quick exit, when she turned all the way around to me, approached me closer and said more "By the way, are you a teacher or some type of speaker?" (At the time I had just started my job at the American Cancer Society and would actually go on to conduct training classes – teaching volunteers – how to work with our constituency, and conducting workshops, teaching men and women how to lessen their risks for receiving a cancer diagnosis.)

What happened next was very surreal in the next few moments as we were standing across from each other, face to face, it seemed that we were the only ones in the room. When I spoke I must have said something about the New Pittsburgh Courier for which I had been freelance writing for a year or so, and maybe something else like procrastination or something, because the next thing I knew she had taken my arm and was walking me around a petition that was in the front of the room, saying, "I feel we need to pray right now against the spirit of procrastination in your life. And she then prayed for me with an intensity that was quite riveting.

When we departed she embraced me she said, "now go get that book done." That was 16 years ago.

Over the years I had a few other similar encounters like this one, not quite as spiritual, but definitely ones that spoke to the vision of a book. The quandary for me was that I never saw myself as one who could create "fiction"; you know the type of stories of love, loss, envy, jealousy, redemption, coming of age tales with the juicy details of teen love, etc. By the same token I was indeed always writing something. Mostly poetry, however, never really telling a story (or so I thought).

That encounter with the evangelist who prayed for me to be rid of the spirit of procrastination, would however set the stage for my unspoken quest for the 'book'. It would not be until after I had taken a writing class at a local University, however, that I would embrace the notion that indeed maybe there would be a book within me. By this time 2007, I was well into *Softer Side Seminars* as my "side endeavor" and had taken a writing class on creative nonfiction just to see if I could.

At the end of the class we had to submit a portfolio that contained all of the material we worked on during the class. I had written some poems about living in Cleveland, and we were asked to create a two page dialogue that we had with another person, we had to write a description of a person's physical self and what their make up was in relationship to the personality you experienced with them.

I had gone through a particularly stressful divorce and was still marveling at how dysfunctional this guy was; this is the material I would use for my portfolio. Speaking of the spirit of procrastination, because of all my outside drama, I did not complete the portfolio until almost two semesters later. I was quite fortunate to have as a professor a woman who had herself been a "non-traditional" student, and had struggled with her own issues around returning to school; so she happily received the late portfolio.

The note I got from her about it was stunning, a real shocker (I kept it for posterity). She first commended me for sticking with this, she told me she knew how challenging it was to continue working on something even though it's life span had passed, then she said the work I submitted reminded her greatly of "Rita Dove"!!! This was well before the encounter with the evangelist.

Still there was no real movement to get busy writing on my part because when I attempted to reconvene my education I changed schools, and entered into a communications program. Low and behold when I did come to my senses and begin to seriously look at writing as something I needed to pursue—who was my intro to poetry instructor?—That same woman; how's this for clarity?

I literally stumbled into Creative Non-fiction and it all began to make sense. It was an immediate love fest between Creative Non-fiction and myself. I found I really enjoyed telling the stories connected to the various phases of my life. One such story "Stepping Outside Kiddieland", I submitted for a competition, and ended up being the first place winner.

I believe that sealed it for me—I have written volumes of essays about my experiences in those three classes including; *Summers in Cleveland, The Soho Chronicles, The House on Pasadena Avenue, The Lessons of Emerald City, Once Upon a time When I Turned 50* and a few more.

But in the meantime I had been writing volumes and volumes of motivational stuff around the Softer Side Seminars Program. Because by the time I won the competition with the Kiddieland story, I was about 2 or 3 years into the annual *Woman to Woman* events. This material always seemed fresh to me, no matter how much time had passed. The Empowerment Program, Softer Side Seminars which I started in 2003, was just about 6 years old.

Thus the information between the pages of this book speak to that time, they speak to the issues that we addressed in all of our sessions and seminars, (well many of them). Also I adopted Jeremiah 29: 11 as the unspoken theme for every workshop I do. "For I know the plans I have for you declares the LORD, plans to prosper you and not to harm you, plans to give you hope and a future." I found this scripture one that gives me peace when I am feeling the most troubled, confused and dismayed about why my life wasn't going anywhere. I believed in "the Plan", but I knew it took work, so I put a picture of that 'work' between these pages.

I believe in my deepest heart of hearts that this is part of "the Plan" God has for my life to bring me to a good end; it is indeed the work I've been called to do. And I do it as I hammer out the knots in my gnarled up life and sandpaper down the rough places these words come—to teach, to admonish, to encourage, to inspire, up lift and to give hope—99.9 percent of it is for ME.

FOREWORD

NOTES FROM THE SOFTER SIDE

Renee Aldrich is my friend. We met several years ago while working on a project together for a local area nonprofit organization. I was immediately struck by her eloquence, her joy and her sparkle. It wasn't long after we met, that she began to tell me about her vision for Softer Side Seminars. It sounded fantastic, but then again, everything Renee talks about sounds fantastic. Whether it's writing an uplifting series of newspaper articles about young future leaders, working with those experiencing homelessness, or attending one of the city's many cultural events, she shares it with passion, and her devotion to all that she cares about is evident.

I am honored to write this foreword because while it can be easy to become frightened as a result of the uncertain times in which we live, Renee instead generously shares her vision of empowerment.

While others are overcome by what seems to be the enormity of grief and pain all around us, she relentlessly seeks a solution. With the heart of a poet and the soul of a warrior she continuously gathers the courage to find joy, to inhale joy, and to share that joy.

But more than simply sharing her joy, in sharing Notes from the Softer Side, my friend strives to elevate, encourage, and inspire us to transcend all that binds us, all that leaves us jaded and broken and reach for something greater within ourselves. The message in Notes from the Softer Side is a message of love founded in a deliberate kindness for ourselves first which can only then successfully spill over to others. With each note, the reader gains insight into their own light. With each note, Renee calls on us to embrace our softer side and recognize that we are worthy of more than we allow ourselves to ever imagine.

I want to live in the world that Renee imagines for us all. A world where we strive to lift each other up... where we seek to find only the good in each other... a world where there is less judgment and more loving. Notes from the Softer Side is the roadmap to that world. That journey begins when we learn to love ourselves. Renee serves as our guide, our guru, our shaman. Notes from the Softer Side guides us to a place of love for ourselves and love for each other.

As the Executive Director of an area Crisis Nursery, I am repeatedly reminded of the need for a kinder and gentler world. In my role, I encounter so many that are isolated, afraid, and battered by overwhelming challenges. Every day I hear a story that breaks my heart and yet every day I am inspired by the resiliency of those in seemingly insurmountable situations who are driven by something greater than themselves. That something greater is always love. Notes from the Softer Side is a tribute to that spirit and that is why I am honored to write this foreword. I am humbled to be even a small part of this inspiring and encouraging endeavor. Read it, embrace it, live it - you will be better for it and the world will be better for it too! Enjoy this journey to self-discovery and love.

LouAnn Ross, MPPM, MAEd
Executive Director of Jeremiah's Place

ACKNOWLEDGEMENTS

One of the drawbacks of thanking people is that invariably when you begin naming names, you run the risk of leaving some out. I don't want to do that. But I feel compelled to make sure I mention folks who did play a significant role in my writing which has resulted, among other things, in the completion of this project.

I want to mention my late great Aunt Erin Mitchell, who was the first African American woman I knew who wrote stuff for others to read—the next one was Maya Angelo. And if you are reading this, and if you know me at all, then you know I am not exaggerating, my aunt was absolutely one of the 'greats'. We lost her in October of 2015 and she was a creative jewel.

Not only did she write, her writing included a great deal of commissioned poetry and plays which were produced in her church. She was funny, quick witted, the life of every family gathering, was a woman of extraordinary talents, and at the top of everyone's list—she was essentially everyone's favorite person.

Because she wrote I WRITE!!

Connie Portis, owner of Renaissance Publications, a weekly community newspaper, and Sonya Toyler who was my first editor at the New Pittsburgh Courier, were the first people who paid me to write, and they did so 'sight unseen' they knew nothing about me or my skill or lack there of. Had it not been for this important work on first *Renaissance Publications* and the *New Pittsburgh Courier*, there would have been no confidence to pursue an actual book.

My friend, Dr. Angela Ford who called me in the middle of the Christmas Holiday that December and told me that the *New Pittsburgh Courier* had an add in the paper for freelance writers; and then she insisted that I should call them—I did and that call resulted in an amazing 15 year ride, a multiplicity of stories, interviewing of celebrities like Diane Reeves, Will Downing, The Heath Brothers, Jenifer Lewis, Just to name a few; reviews of awesome productions like "Stomp' numerous theatrical productions produced by local theater companies and so much more.

I would acknowledge too, Mr. Lewis L. Colyar, a poet and author in his own right. In 2003 I found him in painters whites, which indeed were covered with paint. He was at the top of a scaffold smearing on primer at a facility we both worked. I had hired him to paint my house. In the course of our discussions, he revealed to me he liked to write poems, but hadn't written any in 20 years.

Weeks later he shared and actual a poem with me and I was astounded at its quality. I introduced him to a university writers group, and he got fully immersed into his writing.

ACKNOWLEDGEMENTS

He left group after 2 years because he felt they were not advancing the cause of writers. He started his own group the Langston Hughes Poetry Society, he helped several of its members launch books and by 2012 he had published his own book of poems. After I got over the embarrassment and shame of having not done one thing with my writing, I allowed his accomplishments to motivate me. I also allowed his commitment to my success as a writer, speaker, and a woman in general to continue to be a driving force in my life.

My best friend of over 35 years Marci Walker, owner and operator of Madam Walker's Braidery and School, and the Founder of The S.E.L.F. Image awards, who is such an example of what it means to act on your vision, to 'go hard' or go home, and to keep going until you get to the finish line. She always saw in me what I did not see, and never moddie coddled me about it—I love her to the moon and back.

There is acknowledgement due to my family who in the midst of our struggles we KEEP each other, we CLING to each other, and they make me stay regular.

Above all I acknowledge my children Elliott James Lawrence and Karen-Erin Cammille Aldrich have blessed my LIFE with such joy and peace, and with their steadfast commitment to being productive adults. Because they respect themselves and the life they live, I have been freed up to be creative, to write, to serve in community, to work, to support causes

I have believed in, and because they generally conducted themselves throughout their childhood in such a stellar way, I could be directed to the calling on my life without ringing my hands, and being worried about them.

I must by all means express my heartfelt gratitude and thanks to my brilliant and kind and generous Editor, Akia Williams, no words will adequately describe how she has contributed to whatever success I've had as a writer.

I THANK GOD AND PRAISE HIM EVERYDAY for the miracle of my life, one through which I have been able to continue to create opportunities and blessings. I thank him for placing inside of me SOFTER SIDE SEMINARS, AND SUBSEQUENTLY NOTES FROM THE SOFTER SIDE.

LOVING YOURSELF FROM THE INSIDE OUT

The simple message of Softer Side Seminars is one that charges women to enter a softer more loving relationship with themselves. We must do this in order to effect success in any other relationship we have. I thought I'd take a minute and just discuss exactly what it means to say we should love ourselves--from the inside out.

I spoke to a group of girls who were in a program for "girls at risk", and I posed the question to the young women "Do you love yourself?" They all jumped to answer affirmatively. One young lady slouching down in her chair gave me the neck spin and eye rolled comment. *"Hmph" I know I love myself and I think of myself the most"*. When I asked her how she knew she loved herself, and exactly what did she think it meant -- she gave me an even cockier answer. *"I just do that's all, I know cause I don't let nobody mess w'me"*.

Unfortunately, this idea is not that far removed from some of the adult women who have been in my groups. They often mistake loving themselves with binge shopping, making sure they dress in the most expensive high end clothing they can find, or making sure they go to work telling everyone who will listen about their accomplishments, who they know (there is a lot of name dropping that goes on when folks are operating from an insecure place) or they just go on and on adnauseum giving general information about themselves.

Has anyone ever asked you a question about something you are doing, and before you get your response out, they take over talking about the issue that is most pressing to them? And you then find yourself sitting there 20 minutes later listening to perhaps all the success they are having with that issue??

This is a case of "mistaken identity." These individuals identify this behavior or interaction as signs that they love themselves, but truly it is a sign of their extreme feeling of inadequacy or even insecurity. When you truly feel good about who it is you are, when you are comfortable in your own skin, you do not have to constantly promote your own life to people. As we face our insecurities as women, accept them and realize they do not define us, we then do not feel compelled to make every conversation all about us. You understand that it is not necessary, because folks will find out about you layer by layer--you won't have to say a word. I know a lady who is quite accomplished, and every time she met a man those initial conversations were spent giving him the blow by blow overview of all the amazing things she has done with her life and continue to do. Needless to say this, along with other compatibility issues, things would often NOT come together to create a good jumping off point for building a relationship.

LOVE of self that comes FROM the inside will result in an astute understanding that we do not have to talk about ourselves 24-7. When self love is present, our comfort level is such that we are free to hear another woman's story or perspective. We understand that being a good listener is one of the great tools of relating to others. When we can uplift people by listening to them and at the same time, we uplift ourselves.

Former Editor in Chief of Essence Magazine, Susan Taylor, wrote a piece after doing research on relationships. In this article she shared that in creating the kind of love relationship we want; we would do well to remember that men, often in their quest for love, need to SEE as well as HEAR that the woman of their heart is listening to them. You cannot be listening to YOUR man if you are going on and on and on non-stop about the super woman that is you. Be assured, first of all that if you are super and wonderful, it will slowly and easily and peacefully be revealed to him.

EMBRACE THE SOFTERSIDE --LOVING YOURSELF FROM THE INSIDE OUT --Its better that Way...

"You Can Search The Whole World Over, Underneath Every Nook And Cranny, Behind Every Door And Under Every Crevice Trying To Find Someone Better To Love Than Yourself ----And You Won't Find Them Anywhere Outside The Mirror!!!"

We Are Called To Enter A Softer More Loving Relationship With Ourselves As Women -What Exactly Does This Mean?

That for too long we have been trapped in a cycle of guilt from past mistakes, low self esteem, and feelings of inadequacies. We believe the negative identifiers that others often use to describe us.

We don't believe that we can rise out of our situations, the main reason we don't believe we can, is because we have convinced ourselves that we do not deserve to be in a better place in life.

We allow ourselves to be abused by others, and we add to the abuse by placing their needs above ours.

When we enter into a softer more loving relationship with ourselves, we break those myths, we accept ourselves, flaws and all, understanding that it is not only okay to be flawed, but we won't get out of life with being flawed in some way.

When we enter a softer more loving relationship with ourselves, we forgive ourselves for past mistakes, no matter how large or small, and we come to understand that forgiveness is the first step towards healing.

When we enter a softer more loving relationship with ourselves, our personal well-being is not only our first priority but we understand that unless "we put on our own mask first", it will be impossible to assist anyone else. Additionally we will keep in mind that every time we place our own needs last, we jeopardize the lives of our loved ones.

When we enter a softer more loving relationship with ourselves, we give ourselves permission to excel, positioning ourselves to find our wings and take flight. We understand that moving our lives to the next level is what God intended for us as his perfectly imperfect creation. We come to understand that we have a very clear purpose for being here; and are not intended to lead stagnant unproductive lives.

The What -- The Why -- The Where -- The When and The Who of Self Esteem

Self Esteem refers to the level of belief in, and love you have for yourself. If you have self esteem this means you recognize your value, as a child of God who is perfectly imperfectly made, said as such because in our imperfection God made us perfectly.

Someone asked me once, "where does self esteem come from?" A better question is "how is self esteem developed?" When we are born we enter this world with a blank page. There is nothing on it. We don't have a clue about ourselves, and do not know if we are good, bad or in-between. By the time we begin having a sense of our own existence we start to get feedback from our immediate environment; which includes: parents, aunts, uncles, other relatives or key persons involved in our development from birth until just before we go off to school. This feedback usually goes something like this -- *Oh, she is so cute* or *what a bad little girl* or *your hair is so nappy that I can't do nothing with it* or *she is so pretty, look at her good hair.* Even worse, if we are African Americans, it may go like this *She is so pretty, hmm if only she wasn't so dark.* All these things we may have heard and more. At this point, that once empty page starts to fill up with things that begin to define us, and most of these things on our page come straight from the perspective of others.

As time passes, we get more exposure to the world which was either parents, siblings or others directly involved in our infant and toddler care, and we hear even more things about ourselves. Some of those previous comments are confirmed, and sometimes new things are added. If you add to the equation the fact that others' opinions of us, which end filling up our page, are usually unsolicited and are many times clouded by their own personal baggage and/or unresolved issues. This is demonstrated in a line in the song "Do Nothing Till You Hear From Me', which goes like this *"Why people tear the seams of any one's dream is over my head"*. Who knows what people have been through that creates in them the need to malign others?

By the time we become adolescents and our page is a little more than half full; our peers become more important to us, we discover the opposite sex and the dreaded media. All of these enter our lives and the position of our self esteem is at greater risk as we begin the "am I good enough?" dance. Between the confused state that adolescence often leaves us in, the signals from the media, peer pressure and a natural inclination to seek the attention of the opposite sex; we begin to get lost in society's definition of "good enough", pretty enough, thin enough, light enough, tall enough, and so on and so forth.

And in the absence of an extremely supportive home environment, a place where there is encouragement, nurturing and teaching, that somehow counters the daily onslaught of "why aren't you good enough" messages, by the time we are 25 years old our slate is now loaded with everyone else's concept of who we are and whether or not we are valuable or not; and at this point we begin to buy into it. We believe the smears on our slate that don't empower us and we subsequently begin to act out on that belief. Many times there are other things in our past that increase the way we quickly internalize the negative things that have been drummed into us. As our own opinion of ourselves decreases because of some poor decisions we've made, which are tainted by this poor sense of self, we become vulnerable to abusive relationships. Often we put up with being disrespected in general, as we stay in unrewarding jobs and relationships because we don't believe we deserve better. Additionally we engage behaviors that will validate some of what our page says about us.

> *When I was 19 I was involved in a program which was sponsored by a local corporation and the Kaufmanns Department store. This program was designed to be a refresher course for Black Women who had taken secretarial courses but had not been in jobs where they were using these skills, but also an effort on the part of the Corporation to provide a program that would increase the diversity within their company. The days*

in the twelve-week program were broken up with the morning being devoted to English, grammar and literature and the afternoon was spent drilling on short hand and typing. At the end of the program, out of the 35 girls, some would be accepted into the PPG typing pool, which was pretty much a "cream of the crop" job at that time in the late 60's early 70's. They had very strict guidelines and not everyone would be able to make the cut. Those who were not accepted, however, were guaranteed assistance in going to another company.

At the end of the 12 weeks, participants were tested-- Typing mastery needed to be 60 wpm and the shorthand needed to be 120 words a minute. At the end of this time I, unfortunately, was not successful and came short of the short hand requirement and completely bombed on the typing requirement necessary to be accepted at PPG. Each of us learned of our fate during a meeting with the Corporate Human Resources Representative along with a young African American Social Worker. The HR rep was kind and understanding and assured me that a test is not a determining factor truly on your competency. Not so of the young African American Social worker. I was extremely embarrassed and quite shaken that I had not met those minimum standards. And of course I felt inept and diminished as this African American Woman proceed to affirm my feelings of incompetence.

This woman who had sat during the meeting glaring at me the entire time in a very disdainful manner said as nasty as she could, "I don't know why you are crying, you had to know you weren't cutting it. You probably didn't even try, I know the instructor gave you two trys the taking the test, but you still didn't pass. Even if we place you, I can't imagine that you'll hold the job very long—or any other one for that matter." When she was done, literally berating me (the Human Resources Representative, who was white, sat there red-faced and clearly embarrassed for me) I sat there afraid to stand up. It took me close to 20 years to recognize how I had allowed her comments to live inside of me and wreak havoc on my work life during most of that time. I believed her, she was a trained professional and I was a 20 year old who was just making my way—hadn't even been introduced to my skills or self worth.

This is our charge as mothers, grandmothers, mentors, aunts, and sisters; to make sure those young women who are in our charge are empowered. We must make sure that they know that they are capable, competent, and even gifted, and that nothing anyone says about them can take away from this. But it starts with strengthening our own sense of self.

As women we are called to enter a softer more loving relationship with ourselves. We must refuse to accept whatever negative identifiers we've listened to (forced or otherwise) all of our lives. We can recreate the way we see ourselves and therefore the way we think about ourselves. These two things together can impact our objective for inner peace, joy in our existence, belief that we are endowed by God to be golden achievers and a reflection of his beauty.

****

The role self love plays in our life is powerful

---Without it we continually search for love, validation, approval, and reassurance outside ourselves.

EIGHT NOTES FROM THE SOFTER SIDE

- NOTE #1 FIND YOUR WINGS
- NOTE #2 DROP THE DRAMA
- NOTE #3 QUIT PRETENDING – LOOSE THE MASK!
- NOTE #4 GET OVER THE PAST
- NOTE #5 AVOID HOSTILE CONFRONTATIONS
- NOTE #6 MAKE THAT CHANGE
- NOTE #7 TRAVEL WITHOUT BAGGAGE
- NOTE #8 THE BATTLE IS NOT YOURS

HAVE YOU FOUND YOUR WINGS? ARE YOU FLYING?

Have others recognized a gift in you and been encouraging you to go for it? Do you sometimes feel a yearning to pursue that thing that you love to do that comes natural to you?

- Have you been sitting in a job that you keep because you are afraid to move out of your comfort zone—even though you get depressed every Sunday night when you know Monday is coming?

- Are you still living safely at home with your parents even though you certainly earn more than enough to afford your own place? In the meantime you tolerate daily arguments with your mother on subjects ranging from your desire for more privacy, to her questions about your decisions and the hours you keep, rather than map out a strategy and a financial plan that will allow you to move.

If the answer to any of the above questions is "yes", yet you continue to hold out not making any movement towards change; then I would suggest that you are not "flying". You are operating just underneath the radar screen, afraid to take the leap to the 'next level' of your life. Many of us have not discovered that we have wings, or we know we have wings, but just don't know how to start using them. Some of us have gotten discouraged by a negative incident or person and are stuck in complacency and believe there is no benefit in trying to take flight.

As women we often find ourselves facing any of the above situations. These are barriers, and they steal our courage, keeping us from exploring our capabilities, recognizing our gifts and using them. Unfortunately, the result is that too often it is sometime years before we gain the confidence to spread our wings.

I know of this first hand because –

I was a secretary for over 20 years—and not a very good one. It did not occur to me to even try to do anything different. I even told myself that I loved being a secretary or administrative assistant—it was easier to believe I loved the work knowing I was only mediocre at it, than it was for me to do what it took to discover what I could do and do excellently. I had been trained and therefore had the basic skills that a secretary needed; I could type, take shorthand, make travel arrangements. I also knew how to handle phone calls and greet people. But one of the most vital pieces of being a secretary or administrative assistant was being organized and keeping a boss organized; and this was a major challenge for me. Keeping up with files, and staying on task were two other aspects of being a secretary in which I fell through. Subsequently I did not get good reviews or evaluations, as a result of that, I began to feel inadequate and developed very low self esteem.

Secretarial work paid well (especially in Washington, DC), so after I married and had children it was nice to have the contribution to my family's income. Yet, the income still did not help me feel confident in my abilities, consequently I generally did not have the expectation that I could be better at this work. So I made lots of mistakes, and would make myself nervous by trying to hide the mistakes. The more I did wrong the less I thought of myself. I also felt my employers I had thought the same.

It never occurred to me that the reason I did not do well in the secretarial business was because there was something else I should be doing. Even though I had outstanding skills in other areas (which is why I was able to keep the jobs) I did not see them as enough to make me outstanding. I had great customer service skills, I was a good writer and speller; often I would be asked my opinion on how things could be worded better in the context of a letter or a report—still I only focused on the things I did wrong. Subsequently I would leave the jobs to find another job with the same dynamics, and I always used my own negative thoughts about my performance to complete the same self-fulfilling prophecy and vicious cycle for myself.

In the meantime, friends were always telling me that I was very good with people, easy to talk to, a good writer and speaker; and in church I was always selected to MC programs, give Welcomes and Thank You speeches. Still I stayed in that negative pattern for years, every job I had I would convince myself that I wasn't going to do well, so I didn't.

Finally through the help and encouragement of a mentor, I joined a woman's group while working at a University and begin to see some possibilities in my gifts. Not too long after, I began getting encouragement to apply for other jobs and to see myself functioning on a different level.

It is quiet odd that I slowly begin to gain confidence in my ability to branch out, but it was only after I lost my job at the University because of a bi-polar devious, basically unkind Lead Secretary in my office. It was my intention to sit out from work all summer, and collect unemployment compensation. However, I got a job at a local newspaper, and I started to do some freelance writing. By the end of that summer and into the fall and winter, I had applied for and ultimately secured a position as a community health educator for a national not for profit health organization.

The skills I did not previously recognize as valuable, were instrumental in me receiving nine awards during the 10 years I worked for the organization.

The key to finding our wings and getting in position to take flight is in recognizing ourselves as specially gifted creations of God with unlimited possibilities for our lives.

When I found my wings they were corroded over for lack of use and I had to work hard to get them shined up again and operating smoothly. When I found the courage to take flight, I was astounded to discover the depth of possibilities that exist for me.

Do not let years go by before you 'try your wings'. Close your ears to the negative self talk. Be open to accepting the reality of your gifts. There is a saying that goes 'do what you love and the money will come'.

Too often in our community we have been indoctrinated to the fact that we must get jobs, earn a living, seek after lucrative employment; we are not taught to seek our passions and pursue them. Consequently we get on a tract that leads us to an income, unfulfilled, we get locked into careers and find ourselves there 20 years wondering what happen to 'excellence'.

Dust off your wings—take flight to your future.

For we are God's handiwork created in Christ Jesus to do good works, which God prepared us in advanced to do; Ephesians 2:10

MISSION 1 — TO FIND YOUR WINGS

Your mission should you choose to accept
it is to **spread your wings – take the leap
towards the place you were meant to be**.

Consider acting on something you've been wanting to do; get out of your 'sameness', -- A woman entering a softer more loving relationship with herself understands that loving yourself involves having the heart to develop yourself, using your God given gifts to maximize herself. The better you are for yourself and to yourself, the better you can be to others.

Tips on pursuing this month's mission:

- Pray for Guidance

- Map out a strategy to begin

- Seek a Mentor

- Research your options

- Prepare your environment for whatever impact the change may have START TODAY

ACTION STEPS — FINDING YOUR WINGS—AND TAKING FLIGHT

1. Whatever your project or endeavor to move your life to the next level; whether it is to move out of mom's house, go back to school, start a savings account, enter a fitness program; clean up your credit or downsizing and getting some of the clutter out of your home (This could be keeping you from flying for sure). There is a process that can help you get started. The following are some prompts and action statements to get things moving.

OVER THE NEXT SIX MONTHS TO A YEAR I WANT TO:

(Identify here the project or effort you'd like to complete that will get you in *flight* position)

_____

_____

_____

I WILL BEGIN THIS EFFORT IN A SPECIFIED TIME FRAME

1. TWO WEEKS FROM NOW   DATE: _____
    THREE WEEKS FROM NOW   DATE: _____
    ONE MONTH   DATE: _____
    OTHER   DATE: _____

Note: Don't recommend longer than a month; unless some extenuating circumstance prevents you from a sooner start date—If you put it off a month, it is subject to go in to two, three, four and then never.

2.   Once started, devise a time line to completion or near completion

- By three months from now (start time) I expect

  _____

  to have happened

- By six months from now I expect

  _____

  to have happen

- By the end of the year I expect

  _____

  to have happen

3.   List the names of five people whom you know are already doing, or have already done what you are pursuing. You don't have to know them well, be friends, or even be super acquainted. Put a strategy for connecting with them into your time line; exp. You may aspire to return to school for a degree in

nursing. There is someone in your circle or connected to someone in your circle who has done this as a non-traditional student. Connect with them; be honest, just say you'd like to meet for coffee to hear how they went about going back to get their nursing degree.

If this seems out of the box, well then it is and so be it. If we do not overcome our fear of stepping away from traditionalism our progress will be stilted. And what is the worse thing that can happen? That you reach out and the person does not respond, you then check them off your list and go to the next idea.

Another idea if you are just having trouble making a connection is to call the local school you are thinking about attending talk with an admissions counselor and ASK THEM TO CONNECT THEM WITH SOMEONE WHO IS DOING WHAT YOU WANT TO DO. Those are in bold letters because I can't stress enough the importance of getting the visual of your dream to turn it into your reality.

ELIMINATE THE DRAMA—FOR IT WILL ROB YOU OF YOUR PRODUCTIVITY

"Some people create their
own storms, then get mad when it rains"

In this day and age, it seems like "Drama" is a luxury we run to instead of running away from. Drama unfortunately is that addicting thing that is at the same time insidious and creeps its way into your life sometimes loudly, with a great bang, and sometimes quietly. Then one day you look up and you are so caught in other people's empty drama, your friends, family, co-workers and your own, that you have not accomplished one thing to create the life you deserve.

There is a reason we as women chase drama. It is a great hiding place—when we hide behind drama we do not have to do the work that it takes to take care of ourselves. If we are hiding behind the drama of other people's lives, we let months, days, years go by not focusing on what in the deepest part of our hearts we know we ought to be doing.

Young girls between the ages of 12 and 16, essentially engage drama because it is their "work" per se, it is all they have to do, it is what brings excitement to their lives.

Between the ages of 16 and 18 it is basically the same thing except that the drama heightens and involves more serious issues, of course; such as relationships, the dynamics around break-ups, and depending upon what is going on in the household there very well could be drama among siblings, with parents.

If drama is in your life at the age of 35 years old, YOU ARE HIDING. What does drama look like?

At work: There is a colleague who is always trapping you in the ladies room with the 411 on what management is doing and how they are doing it, this co-worker thrives on the shocked looked on everyone's face or how she can send folks into a panic with her so called first hand news –

At home among siblings: You have three sisters and your one sister (maybe the youngest or sometime it is the oldest) is always in "moms" ear, but she then calls each one of you individually with a "twist" on the way the story went, get's everyone incited until there are a couple different variations on the story.

Among Friends: You find out your good friend's man is carrying on in a flirtatious manner with another of your friends in the circle, the buzz starts and is kept going until in a dramatic explosion it all hits the fan, the girlfriend finds out, she finds out that you knew and the others knew as well, and it goes round and round until the next dramatic episode.

If in fact you are caught up in the embroiled mess, added to it, helped to keep it going then you are part of the drama. If these scenarios are ones you engage, and help to keep going you may be hiding from some productive endeavor.

I recall going to an open house at a local university, this is after contemplating going back to school for many years. When I finally went to this open house I was excited and eager. Regrettably, three years passed when I accidentally found the papers I filled out at the open house, I still hadn't enrolled in school. When I saw those papers I felt the gut wrenching jolt in my stomach that said "You've' been hiding!" Now it may or may not have been behind drama in the sense of the above scenarios but in the drama associated with personal procrastination, with self doubt which kept me doing other less meaningful things, with relationships that I knew when I entered them they were not going anywhere. Either way I spent my time, effort and energy, and on tons of random things (including helping others with major projects they were working on) that ultimately were not leading to progress of my life. Subsequently almost ten + years later I entered into the University as a non-traditional students and at the time of this writing am still about 15 months out. But at least I'm on track

As we enter a softer more loving relationship with ourselves we recognize how important our time is. We recognize the places that rob us of our energy and that have the capacity to leave us in an empty unproductive place.

Rejecting the drama of others, ridding ourselves of the habit of creating drama, will leave us with a clear head, with focus on our goals and prospective, and leave us with energy to proceed—to GET IT DONE

Your Mission Should You Choose To Accept
It Is To Step Away From The Brain Draining,
Productivity Stealing Drama In Your Life –
And The People Who Bring It

—Be on the lookout for the pitfalls of drama and those who chase after it; be careful not to lose your focus and get off track if you are on a mission—to enter a softer more loving relationship with yourself.

Tips for Backing Out of Drama, Avoiding it, and Drama Queens and Kings

-- Stay Alert or conscious when something belongs to someone else—leave it with them
-- Keep focus on where you want to be
-- **<u>WORK PLACE</u>** Drama is very dangerous, don't be involved by spreading rumors – wait until information comes from upper management before you respond or react

-- **<u>FAMILY DRAMA</u>** – Don't let sisters, cousins, your mother or brother carry tales to you. Be strong and resist the urge to feed into "guess what he or she said about you" If something comes to you, let it stop with you. Family Drama is a tough one because we are most vulnerable in the place where love is. It is important to recognize where you need to make a space between yourself and that which steals your productivity

-- **CHURCH DRAMA** – We know that this is NO place for Drama, but we also know that we can find it there. Again, resist the urge to join in. Remember why you are there and keep your focus on what you believe your worship should look like.

-- Firmly Step back from the People you know are creating drama and want to pull you in

-- Be committed to the process of YOUR LIFE

-- Be fully committed to safe guarding yourself from the thief that steals your productivity -- DRAMA

ACTION STEPS — BACKING AWAY FROM DRAMA—TAKES BEING INTENTIONAL

Engaging In personal drama and being drawn into other people's drama is perhaps one of life's most unproductive dynamics.

It takes deliberate intention and consciousness to protect your self from getting caught up in other people's drama as well as making sure you avoid personal drama. Developing a defined process for this will help you avoid the hidden traps that leave you ensnared in brain draining drama. Below are some guidelines to help navigate the murky shark filled drama waters.

1. Look out for Key words that are clues that someone is trying to pull you into their drama

2. There certain phrases that drama kings and queens use every day

    A. "Girl you won't believe this"

    B. "OMG" wait until you hear what's about to happen at work."

3. Be alert if others come to you to tell you what someone else said about you. Don't let your sister come and tell

you "Guess what momma said about you"; or even what you other sister said about you.

REGULARLY MAKE THE FOLLOWING STATEMENTS:

I WILL focus on the important issues I need to be dealing with in my life

I WILL not be an open recipient to gossip or on the job scuttlebutt

I WILL Stop Rumor mills and gossip as soon as it gets to me

I WILL Endeavor to keep my home drama Free – AT LEAST ON SUNDAYS

WHO IS THAT MASKED WOMAN? BE YOURSELF

*"Persons of high self-esteem are not driven to
make themselves superior to others; they
do not seek to prove their value by measuring
themselves against a comparative standard.
Their joy is being who they are, not in
being better than someone else."*
"Anonymous"

**One of the overwhelming challenges of being a woman
is coming to terms with who it is we are**; the media hype
about what it means to be beautiful, and what it means to
have a perfect body, leaves us seriously struggling to accept
our physical make up as well as our life condition. Because of
this; we often allow ourselves to be subject to the opinions
of the people in our lives: family, friends, significant others,
and sometime even employers. The problem with this is
that the opinions of others are often formed by whatever
their view is of themselves; and sometimes that view is
warped. Additionally, it has been proven that for too many
years women, in general, have been owned by society. And
this society has dictated to us what we should look like,

sound like, act like, where we should live, and what groups we should belong to, and so much more.

Most assuredly this adds to the pressure to those of us who feel we don't measure up, and that if we don't do something, or act like something society says we should, that we'll just be none existent. Dr. Laure Rosewarne, a notable Austrian Psychologist made the following observation: in the matter of society sees women, *its established that society renders women of "a certain age" invisible and unattractive, i.e. synonymous with a failure to contribute meaningfully to society."* With this kind of standard, unless we as women have a high sense of self, the need to wear a 'mask' will follow us around like a relentless puppy, crying to be put on; "wear me, this mask, because you know you are not good enough as you are."

Then there is the 'self imposed' quest to be perfect. In the work place we go through great lengths to create a picture of perfection, including taking on projects that belong to other people, working extended hours to keep up, and coming to work ill. We generally end up bringing stress and anxiety on ourselves by trying to be indispensable, rather than assessing the reality of our capabilities and then being honest about it.

How exactly does the "Masked Woman" function? A woman wearing a mask meets people and creates an imaginary existence; one that she feels will present herself in a better light. After about five minutes of conversation, she has told all of her business--having exaggerated much of it.

> *[Once when I was working in Washington, DC I lived in a woman's dormitory for government workers. There was this girl, whom we'll call Betty, who used to entertain us in the evening with many stories of her seemingly "perfect life" before, she moved to DC. One of the stories she told was that she was brought to DC by the Department of the Interior and actually started as a Grade 7 (which was an extremely high salary for a Secretary back then.) We were all impressed because securing that kind of salary just entering the government workforce was unheard of). However, as it turned out, we learned that she and I actually worked for the same agency. (and truth be told I had been recruited to DC from Pittsburgh by the State Department) I had been brought in as a Grade 5 because I already had 4 years of experience when I took the civil service exam. Most of the girls in our dorm who also had come from different cities, did not have the experience, and therefore started as Grades 2's or 3's. Since I was a Grade 5 I was identified to join an application review panel in the agency department of personnel. This was a panel brought together to review applications and resumes of people who were seeking promotions or next 'grade level' jobs. It was during one*

of these sessions were the applicants had applied for a job paying a Grade-4 salary, that I discovered that Betty from the dorm had made up much of what she told us about herself.

I was stunned to see that she was not only a Grade-2, but she had been placed on probation for not measuring up to the job requirement at her last review. This girl had also told us she was taking classes at George Washington University and was in a Sociology program. The truth was that she was actually taking a shorthand class so that she could qualify for a grade level increase. I knew this girl for the entire 15 years I lived in DC, and regrettably, she stayed behind the "mask" all of that time. In case you are wondering, no I did not betray "Betty's" secrets. Even though she was a braggart, and always played one ups with each of us, somehow I felt a little sorry for her. I was young, maybe age 22, and not very sophisticated at all, but instinctively I didn't think shaming people would stop them from telling the stories they needed to tell. I did, however, develop a little more savvy when it came to 'hearing' what people were saying and understanding there could be a difference in what they were saying about themselves, and what the truth was.]

A masked woman will engage her friends in a lot of the made up imagery around which she has surrounded

herself. She pretends to have finances which she does not have, going so far as to make major purchases like luxury cars and getting into homes with huge mortagages just so she can appear to her friends to 'have it like that'. She pretends to be more professional than she really is, by engaging in social activities that she really doesn't like, with people she really doesn't like because she thinks it gives her 'points' with people upon whose opinion she places too much importance.

It is in romantic relationships where 'wearing the mask' is often most prevalent, and most dangerous. We enter into romantic relationships projecting a fake persona; then become hard pressed to keep up. Ultimately we generate more anxiety and stress as we become worn down attempting to keep up the facade'.

[*When I married my first husband I so wanted to be the perfect wife and 'servant' to him. When he did not know how he wanted his eggs for breakfast, I would fix a scrambled egg and an over easy egg, and if he was not sure if he wanted home fries or pancakes, I would fix both.*

My aunt admonished me that this was unrealistic. She said "Renee you need to 'start out like you can hold out,' if your marriage is going to last a lifetime. Do you think you will want to cook like this every morning for the next 40 years?" I did not appreciate her wisdom at the time, because I wanted it to look like this was okay with me, even though it was not. My marriage ended in 5 years and much of the reason had to do with me not being true to myself in the beginning.]

Another place where you see a lot of "masked women", unfortunately, is in the church. In our churches we are many times presented with a picture of what our spirituality should look like. For many these guidelines are pretty stringent. So on Wednesdays and Sundays we pretend a pious religiousity that we really can't pull off. We don't receive encouragement to be the best that we can be, and be 'for real' as opposed to holding ourselves up to some man made interpretation of how and/or what our Christian walk should be. I've seen many young women sink into the pits of despair and depression trying to pretend they were something they weren't so they could get the 'nod' of approval from the church mothers who of course never did anything wrong in the entirety of their holy lives.

Paul Lawrence Dunbar wrote *"We wear the Mask that Grins and Lies...why should the world be over-wise in counting all our tears and sighs? We wear the Mask."* Dunbar's reference was the fact that **it was safer for us to pretend in front of white people during slavery.** His poem speaks to the need we had for keeping a masked face—so that our weaknesses, and/or plans would not be revealed. **But, WHY DO WE MASK today?** Again, something that was once necessary to protect us as a people from our oppressors, has been transferred to our interpersonal relationships as we use it as a tool against one another.

More often than not, we mask the truth about ourselves, because we don't believe that we will be appreciated as we are. We believe that we are unacceptable, and we believe this because we do not accept ourselves. We spend so much time finding fault with ourselves, and accepting what it is others deem as unacceptable faults about us, that we start to really believe that we are the sum total of those mistakes and poor choices and nothing more. We fail to realize that the very people we are trying to impress are themselves flawed!!

If we are honest, we'll admit that we have all done some 'masking' at some point in time. The concern is for those who live indefinitely behind a mask. The problem with this is that the masked woman is also living in fear—fear of being found out. Again, fear creates stress, stress creates more anxiety, and both can and often do result in serious physical illness—real or imagined.

A Woman entering a softer more loving relationship with herself, knows that she has been perfectly made by God, flaws, foibles and all. If her flaws are something she wants to work on, she does so on her own terms, but not in response to trying to meet someone elses expectations of her. She, therefore, will realize that pretending to be something she isn't is not necessary. When you meet this woman, you do not meet her 'representative.' Because she finds herself 'acceptable', and meeting her own approval, and will therefore expect that everyone else will too. **She boldly unmasks and says "What you see is what you get", if you are not okay with it, get over it!**

MISSION 3 — DROP THE MASK AND FREE YOURSELF BY BEING YOURSELF

YOUR MISSION SHOULD YOU CHOOSE TO ACCEPT IT IS TO – Drop Mask – Love yourself, accept yourself, honor yourself – not as perfect, but perfectly imperfectly made in the image of God-- TRUST AND BELIEVE, he did not make a mistake with you—Just as you are, you are ENOUGH

ACTION STEPS – Towards DROPPING THE MASK

- Get to **know yourself** you'll be surprised how interesting you are as your true self

- **Develop new interests** and you'll be so busy cultivating them, you won't have time to take the time to hide-- plus it will increase your confidence

- **Lend a hand** to someone who needs it, they'll teach you how to appreciate your true self

- Acknowledge that **this is an issue for you**, and **pray for guidance** in honoring the unique qualities that make the **real you** too special to HIDE behind the Mask

GET OVER IT!!

HANGING IN THE PAST WILL KEEP YOU FROM MOVING INTO YOUR FUTURE

"The brightest future will always be
based on a forgotten past;
you can't really go on well in life until you let go
of your past failures and heartaches," **Anonymous**

The above quote has been said many times, in many different ways. I believe so much so that at this point the words "you must leave the past behind" no longer have as strong a meaning as it once did. It is rather like what happens to young couples when one or the other every weekend has something to apologize for; and the "I'm sorry's" begin to lose some of their steam. Many us know what it is to say, "I'll just have to move on"; but have not really discovered the fine art to 'getting over it'.

Self-help gurus have written books, conducted entire workshops and held seminars on the importance of closing the door on what was, and focusing on what is to be. And while many of us women work hard to convince ourselves and others that we understand this concept and practice it; the truth is, 'letting go" is more than just "saying so".

In fact, getting over past hurts, disappointments and offenses can be extremely difficult. If it weren't, it wouldn't be such an issue for so many people, especially women. I am not saying we are completely unforgiving; actually, that is part of the problem. Many times we want so badly to appear as though some misdeed is not bothering us; we act as though we have forgiven and forgotten when the reality is we haven't really dealt with the issue so that we can freely release it.

We have just tried to bury it and move on. When you do that, invariably it comes back to haunt us in some form. The other extreme to this is that we allow the anger and hatred for someone, or about something, to get deep down inside of us, then we stay 'mad' at that person; perhaps waiting for them to realize how wrong they did us until it eats a hole inside. Again we think we have handled it by just hating, and being angry, but it is still festering within unresolved and 'blocking' the pathway to freedom that forgiveness provides. There is definitely a special consciousness involved in this thing called "getting over the past".

Let's examine why forgetting, forgiving, and moving on is such a struggle. One reason, as strange as it may seem, is that sometime we want to stay stuck in a place of pain. For some, wallowing in that unfair thing that happened to us, gives us a kind of identity that perhaps we are afraid to break free of. In other words, we have such a shabby sense of self, that we fear the freedom to just look at ourselves without the weight of that baggage. We unconsciously know that if we shake off that old stuff, we may have to do something productive and responsible with our lives.

Another reason we lag in our past, is that it is easier to stay, than to invest in the 'work' it would take to climb out. Inability to forgive ourselves is another reason we remain locked in some past event for which we blame ourselves. The challenge of entering a softer, more loving relationship with ourselves is acknowledging our errors, owning the weakness, forgiving ourselves and focusing on the future. This is important because its a fact of life that if we cannot bring ourselves to forgive ourselves, then we won't be able to comprehend the all consuming power of the love of God who stays ready to forgive us, wants to do it, and will do it.

The top reason, however, that we can't get over some of the pain of our past, is the inability to forgive the one who offended us. This is how our past gets in the way of our future. Our anger, bitterness, resentment and sometime rage consumes us, and fills up those places were blessings belong.

We have the notion that forgiving the person who wronged us is saying that "it was okay" what they did. This is a grave misunderstanding. Be assured that the expectation in forgiveness is not that the offender has no accountability, and that we should forgive them, shrug our shoulders and blindly stay targets for repeat offenses. The act of forgiveness is directly related to the appropriate process for moving our lives to the next level. It is seeing a situation for what it is, handling it, and making a self affirming decision to step away from the harm or pain and then not holding on to it.

The act of forgiveness is between you and God mostly; and when in cases were it is feasible, yes, it could mean a verbal declaration to the offending individual. But it is in your heart where it is most important that you make the transition from the anger to peace, this peace comes from understanding that your time, and energy are so much more valuable than to be used obsessing about the terrible event.

[I specifically recall a situation that transformed me. I belonged to an organization where I one day found myself the object of, what I thought at the time, was a terrible conspiracy by a certain individual within the organization to discredit me; and ease me out of a position I held. (it was not a leadership position) I was called on the carpet about some alleged infractions in front of about 10 people—including the head of the organization. Everyone was there with the exception of my accuser—who had submitted a 3 page letter filled with accusations about me. This was in September of 1999, I vividly even now remember the emotion as I sat there listening to these people asking me to essentially defend myself about

the information that was in the letter (which by the way had been written 3 months earlier of the same year). So what I learned on that day in September was that everyone in the meeting had been walking around interacting normally with me all these months (including my accuser) knowing about this letter and that this meeting was coming. I was told that due to scheduling problems it could not be dealt with before 3 months had passed.

I was totally blind sided by this whole thing. While I was definitely aware that, due to transitions within the organization, the accuser and I were butting heads, still, I felt that the respect we had for each other and the fact that we had already been working together indirectly for six years, would provide an opportunity for us to smooth out our issues. I never thought organizational leadership would meet with me to discuss accusations—without the presence of my accuser.

Of course, I chose not to even entertain the idea of defending any of the content of the letter; and of course I immediately resigned from that position. For almost two years I wrestled with this thing, I still tried to remain a part of this organization thinking that I could just move on mentally. But at the end of that time I knew that trying to stay had been a mistake.

I was there, but I lingered in my resentment, I watched as it seemed that no one within the organization had a heart for what I was going through. It was tough to walk in there and not keep getting the visual of the humiliation I experienced on that day. I could not forgive these people nor did I want to forgive them. Until finally the wisdom of an elderly lady friend brought me to the reality of what I had to do. When I kept complaining to her saying that "they had to know how wrong it was of them to do that to me, every one of them, even the head of our organization." She said to me, "People have a way of convincing themselves that they were right about something; you want them to come forward and say they were wrong— and you can just forget that. Waiting on that is what's tearing you up inside—holding on to that hope keeps you the victim. You will stay torn up and confused and miserable as long as you hold on to it. LET IT GO!!" In that instant, I was through, I left that organization and began to systematically forget the incident, and over time I forgave the parties. Subsequent to that, I had doors opening for activities and creative situations that I would not have been able to take advantage of if I was still in that position with that organization].

What I learned from this painful experience was that for every reason people find to hold on to the negative past, there are just as many reasons for letting go. A key reason is that the longer you hold on to the thinking that there is some value in that, the longer it will eat away at you; another important reason it is actually essential to let go, is that the longer you delay the process of moving on, the longer you delay your healing. It is a fact that you cannot progress with an open unhealed wound because when you least expect it, you bang that wound and the pain goes all through you again. And lastly, but most importantly, holding on to those old hurts and anger, does not leave you in a POSITION OF POWER, but it really is a reflection of your POWERLESSNESS. Think about it, in any situation where our physical or emotional power is compromised, we still have free will of our thoughts, and literally can choose to release anything that is holding us as a mental hostage.

Accomplishment in life lies in the free creative flow of our beautiful minds. If our minds are cluttered up with remnants of some distant, unresolved hurt, there is no space for growth. We must keep ourselves open to the blessings intended for us by consciously deciding to step out of this past. Just like I was told by my wise elderly friend, "waiting on someone else to make a past situation right will tear you up inside". The first tool we possess to help us in moving on is our minds and thoughts. Whatever our past experience has been, whatever wounds or heartaches they have rendered to us—We are still in charge of our thinking—this is where our power lies.

MISSION 4—GET OVER THAT PAST STUFF

Your Mission Should you choose to accept it, is to get intentional about letting go of the Past,

- If it hurt, let it go,

- If you are <u>sorry</u>, apologize and let it go,

- If you need to forgive? Do so, and let it go

- and KEEP YOUR FACE AND THOUGHTS IN FRONT OF YOU

TIPS FOR MOVING ON

Quit sharing the story over and over again with friends or family members. (If you need to talk with a professional do so, but don't just keep it as a topic of your conversation in general)--even supporters tire of the broken record you become.

God has provided prayer as a means of communicating with him. Use it in your efforts to let go of past pain.

Go ahead and give yourself permission to be sad, angry, disappointed, disillusioned or whatever you need—PUT A TIME LIMIT ON IT, and then start the process of moving on.

Understand that moving on is a process, and the quicker you begin it, the quicker you get to your healing.

Don't expect it to be easy, but do expect it to be doable—Do not be ashamed or too proud to seek professional help, it is a sign of strength.

KEEP YOUR FACE *always* ⟶ TOWARD THE *sunshine* AND SHADOWS WILL FALL BEHIND YOU. *walt whitman*

FIFTH NOTE

AND THEN THERE'S THE Baggage— Leave it at the Door of New Situations

Start Each morning Fresh and New. God did not create you to carry around all that Baggage, let it go and move forward into the life of Blessing he has in store for you.......Joel Osteen

Many of us are carrying around a boatload of excess baggage and we wonder why we are plodding along through our life instead of sprinting. In the previous "Note" we discussed the importance of not living in the past by holding onto hurt, guilt, or anger of past incidences. Many times when we are successful in getting over our pasts, and we are no longer angry, or no longer have the pain of whatever the hurt was and we do move on; regrettably, there is the tendency to bring the baggage—like not trusting, being on edge, or maintaining a negative attitude. I once had a friend say to me, "I don't even start out believing any one, and then I am not disappointed when I find out they are lying." It is safe to say there is some baggage here.

This baggage weighs us down because it is heavily laden with that past stuff, guilt, or fear of failure based on something that didn't work out in our lives previously, or; as in our example, plain old lack of trust because we've been lied to in the past.

The bags are filled with insecurities and self doubt, so we enter into new possibilities believing we are not good enough. Old baggage is far more detrimental than a fistfight because at least you know you are in a "fight". You can, therefore either put up your dukes and fight back or not—your choice. But baggage is sometime insidious and we are often carrying it around and we aren't even aware of it because it doesn't even manifest itself until we are attempting something new—like a relationship, a job, making a major purchase, starting a fitness program, or even starting a business.

Our shoulders are slumped over from the weight of the baggage. We turn people off by responding to things negatively because of the baggage we bring; we sabotage 'good' relationships, feed into the hype that 'there are no good men' out here because we choose to lug the baggage of a bad romance around with us as opposed to judging each situation on its own merits.

A Woman entering a softer more loving relationship with herself is acutely aware of the damage of baggage. She understands that holding others to a standard based on baggage from her past is counter productive. Part of learning to love yourself is allowing new situations to flourish, see the good in them, and trust that you will be 'okay' even if this new thing isn't "the" thing. By all means be conscious of lessons we should take from past experiences, but do not ascribe actions and outcomes of the past to the new and current situation.

A lesson looks something like this:

> *When I was in my early 20's living and working in Washington, DC, a group of us lived at a housing complex which the Government used when it recruited young women from other cities for employment. I met lots of young women like myself and we formed friendships one or two of whom I am currently still friends. But there were the others whose behaviour was not representative of real friendship. One of them was a chronic liar; one with whom I had developed a close friendship and was sharing information about a guy I was dating, literally was behind my back seeing him; and was telling some of the other girls—and another one borrowed $100.00 from me, money which I had to borrow from my uncle to loan her; and ducked me for months trying not to pay me back. I subsequently had to repay my uncle out of my paycheck and almost ruined my plans to move.*

> *There were other occurrences as well, but the point is I could have placed these things in a suitcase and begin carrying them around with me everywhere; not*

trusting people, thinking everyone was a liar, believing all who profess to be my friend would go after my boyfriend, or I could have really bought into that false notion that women were not good to have as friends. Thank God I got through this stuff, remained hopeful and trusting. Did I learn from these things? Yes; do I still get disappointed sometime by people? Yes, but I'm blessed everyday that I left those suitcases in Hancock Hall and never took them with me into other places.

There are many lessons on our different journeys, lessons to be applied so that we can get back to the business of enjoying life and believing that each experience can be rich in a multiplicity of ways. The inability to this is one of the reasons why we find ourselves "Stuck", "blocked" unable to progress, hampered by a past that has gone on about it's business except for the living space we provide for it in our heads.

MISSION 5 — LEAVE THE BAGGAGE

YOUR MISSION SHOULD YOU CHOOSE TO ACCEPT IT
IS TO UNPACK THOSE BAGS, UNLOAD
YOURSELF OF THE REMANTS OF PEOPLE,
PLACES, AND THINGS, THAT WEIGH YOU DOWN.

TIPS FOR ELIMINATNG THE BAGGAGE

1. Agree with yourself that you need a "Fresh Start" Mental adjustment regarding your need will prepare you for stepping away from your baggage.

2. Look at each new experience on its own merits – give it a chance to be successful—you fail to do this when you enter with the same negative expectation from a previous experience

3. Be intentional!! You cannot leave unpacking to chance -- take control by asking yourself 4 powerful questions

   (1.) Is this that I am holding onto serving me?

   If the answer to this is "No" then unpack it.

   (2.) Have I faced this issue to rid myself of it?

> If the answer to is "No"—then this is the first step to unpacking—take off the blinders you have baggage

(3.) Am I running from it, but getting no where fast?

> If the answer to this is "yes", be assured the more you keep running to get away from the baggage without unpacking it, the more it will chase you.

(4.) I am secretly KEEPING this issue on purpose?

> If the answer to this is "yes", consider seeking professional support to navigate you through and help you unpack this very heavy bag.

4. If possible (and it is possible) separate yourself from the daily reminders of how awful that thing was that happened to you

5. Be consistent, don't give up and get back into relationship with your baggage. Trust the process, it will take time to free yourself, but if you don't take the time you'll never be free

DROP THE HOSTILITY

HOSTILE CONFRONTATIONS – Create more Problems than they solve

"Anger and hatred cannot bring harmony. The noble task of arms control and disarmament cannot be accomplished by confrontation and condemnation. Hostile attitudes only serve to heat up the situation, whereas a true sense of respect gradually cools down what otherwise could become explosive...." Dalai Lama

Stories about fighting, filthy language, actual verbal and/or physical confrontations, boasting about threats that you have hurled at supervisors or family members, reports of having cursed someone out royally--does any this sound like what you would hear in a men's locker room, a pool hall or on a construction site? Perhaps it does, but sadly, these are also sounds you would hear at any given time on the back of a bus filled with young black women between the ages of 18 and 25 (and even younger).

These are manifestations of the hostility that seems to be so pervasive in women in this age group. They erroneously think this is the answer to any challenge they encounter with other people or situations (such as someone bumps into them at the club). I refer to the head snapping, eye rolling, hand on hip, finger waving sisters who think they must exhibit this behaviour in order to be seen, or to display some type of false bravado.(I would offer here that media images in the reality television shows we are bombarded with, filled with depictions of women in constant cat fights and otherwise coming at each other, do not help.)

However, the truth is that most often these actions have more to do with feelings of insecurity and fear of being judged rather than of real anger. Yet, there are times when it is <u>real</u> anger, but the anger is misdirected. It could be distress about being a 22 year old single mom of 2, you have no diploma or GED so you are stuck at a menial job and do not see your way out. Perhaps the anger is at the boyfriend who, now that you are 7 months pregnant, is frequently seen at the club with his new conquests, and he has not phoned you in two weeks.

While these are legitimate problems, unfortunately they are not legitimate reasons to snap at everyone you come into contact with, walk around with a chip on your shoulder, or if you are fortunate enough to have a job, go to work every day with the *"I want to fight"* look on your face. At the end of this behaviour, the problem is not fixed and things are most likely worse, because you've probably managed to alienate those closest to you..

Make no mistake, this is not a phenomena relegated to younger women. I have had many negative experiences with angry confrontational women of color over 45 years of age. I can site two separate incidences with women in the workplace.

> [*The first was years ago when I worked at an association in Washington DC with a woman we will call Barbara. The other was about 12 years ago with a woman we will call Anita, while working in a Senior Administrators office at a University. Both of these women had been in their jobs in excess of 15 years, both were very capable and worked hard. I was a new employee in both cases and an easy target for their disdain. Both Barbara and Anita were deeply resentful of my presence because the hiring process was mishandled by management. Barbara in DC had been in her position as receptionist with this Association for quite a number of years. She did not have the skill set and therefore had been passed over for the executive assistant job three times when I was brought in. Meanwhile at the University, I was recruited and hired to be a back up to Anita, an Executive Assistant to a senior staff member; and she (Anita) had not been allowed to participate in the selection process.*
>
> *No doubt they both had cause to feel disrespected and angry, but I should not have been the target of their*

resentment. At the Association it was particularly problematic because although Barbara lacked the advanced skills necessary to do the job, she did have many years with the company and she knew her work very well. Ours was a small office and we had to work closely together -- she made my life miserable simply because she could. She did not direct her anger to the management who had overlooked her for years (and who were all white males mind you) nor did she elect to seek other employment. At the University, ultimately it took an intervention from another senior administrator to influence a change in Anita's behaviour towards me; but not without much wailing and gnashing of teeth.]

It is important to note here, that I had such an unhealthy sense of self in both situations, that my misery was increased because I didn't even attempt to stand up for myself in either case.

Historically Black women have had to be every thing to everyone, we've had to keep families together, raise children alone, work as domestics in factories, restaurants, and/or other low paying or demeaning jobs just to keep a roof over their heads. There have been instances when we've had to stand strong with husbands, being a source of support and strength when they (the husband) have had to endure adverse situations. Therefore it became necessary for us to take on a stalwart posture with a no nonsense attitude 'ready to take on anything potentially threatening to our family environment.

Somehow over the years that demeanour which we once needed to protect and advance our families and show support to our spouses, has been transferred and embraced by some young sisters and held on to by many older sisters, and the results have not been positive. The dynamic has changed so that instead of a tool to 'guard' us from very real adversaries, that fighting spirit and hostile posture has become a weapon we use against each other, and a place behind which we hide our insecurities, fears and inadequacies.

It has been said in so many ways that engaging in hostile confrontations rarely works. It is ineffective in the work place, and it places your employment at risk It does not work in families; we know that siblings go for years of not speaking to each other about incidences that can rarely be remembered. It does not work with adult children, if you've done your job you should not need to 'get into it' with another grownup, if they are minor children then there should be no back and forth argument anyway. Most assuredly it does not work with spouses, ask yourself when is the last time a huge confrontation resolved anything with him or her? Most importantly, when we allow ourselves to be drawn into pointless argumentation—WE GIVE AWAY OUR POWER!!

Be assured that the idea is not that we should be doormats for others, be they spouses, employers, children, siblings, family or friends; nor is this to suggest that we should walk around with a perpetual grin on our faces or that we will not be challenged by the behaviour of others towards us. The hope is that we learn to position ourselves so we are not drawn into hostile confrontations. It is important to map out a strategy that will remove you from such situations before they start. We do have choices in all matters and if we do not have choice of what the other person is doing, we do have the choice of how we react

A Woman entering a softer more loving relationship with herself, recognizes the importance of preserving her mental and physical health by choosing to avoid ugly, hostile confrontations. She knows that it is healthier to deal with a situation in a manner that will affect results—major confrontations make complicated matters even more complicated. When we love ourselves we want the best for ourselves, we are then satisfied to 'rest' in our correctness, chose our battles, and then approach the battle to get results. Additionally, we have enough security and sense of self to not make scenes, or be drawn into scenes to prove any point to anyone.

MISSION 6—DROP THE HOSTILITY

YOUR MISSION SHOULD YOU CHOOSE TO ACCEPT
IT IS TO COMMIT TO DROPPING THE HOSTILITY,
QUIT BEING SO REACTIONARY –
EVERY BATTLE IS NOT YOUR BATTLE

TIPS FOR DROPPING THE HOSTILITY

1. Own your "stuff" you know if you engage in pointless hostility, are quick to blow up and always ready for a fight. This may be challenging—it takes being very honest with yourself—which can be painful; but the subsequent freedom is remarkable

2. Think about this issue every day

3. Be intentional!! This is one transition you cannot leave to chance.

4. Think about past incidences, play them back in your mind, and redesigned what your responses should have been

5. Life is about Choices -- CHOOSE TO NOT FIGHT—It is very unattractive and hard on the heart

6. As in many areas of transformation—Do not be ashamed to seek help—Seeking help makes sense when you are struggling.

IT BEGINS WITH YOU—
MAKE THAT CHANGE

"Only when we love ourselves completely do we understand our value – We understand it enough to make the necessary changes, in our lives for all the right reasons."
Renee P. Aldrich

Mahatma Gandhi, the premier spiritual leader of India, who would ultimately lead his people to their independence from England through the execution of civil disobedience, urged his followers to "be the change you seek in the world". Michael Jackson had a terrific hit in the late 80's whose lyrics held the same premise. "I'm looking at the man in the mirror, I'm asking him to change his ways."

The challenging question of today is **why is it that we feel that we must go around trying to change everyone else in order for things in our lives to be correct or to work out?**

We enter into relationships with a plan in mind to change something we do not like about the other person. We relate to family members the same way, telling ourselves that things would be better in the family if only my brother, mother, sister, father would just change. We actually say, if THEY would just change their ways, things would be so much better.

Here are the facts--people do not change, they are what they are. Either we can handle it, or we can't. When it comes to other people, we can try to influence their thinking, or offer advice only if it is solicited, but we cannot fix people nor change them. They can only fix or change themselves. We try to change people because we often have lofty expectations of them. As such, what we forget is that they are human just like we are, and more than likely they will not live up to that expectation.

The lesson, herein, is to minimize our expectations of others, and expect the most from ourselves. If we do so, then we'll be so busy trying to master that, that we won't have time nor energy trying to make another person be something we want them to be. Anytime we enter any situation expecting to change the other person, we are setting ourselves up for failure. Instead we should try learning to accept people for who they are, and wherever we see the need for an adjustment, make it within ourselves.

A Woman entering a Softer more Loving Relationship with herself understands that is what change is, it's an inside job. Begin on the inside, with 'you', and the air around you will take care of itself. It is not easy, but it is doable. Understanding that you only have the power to change yourself, and not others is the key to peace. It is also freeing because when you understand that you have no control over others, and you are no longer trying to change them, you will begin to use that energy to work on YOU, finding that you are disappointed less.

MISSION 7—CHANGE BEGINS WITH YOU

Your Mission Should you Choose to Accept it is to Spend some introspective time with your self, examine any shorts you feel may be keeping you from your destiny – and execute the courage to make that CHANGE

Tips to making that change

Five Steps to change

1. Recognize the need in you!

2. Quit saying "I can't change, this is just who I am"

3. Be patient with yourself this won't happen over night

4. Pray in earnest for God's guidance and direction

5. Don't wait until tomorrow-- "right now change" begins today.

There is a profound lesson in the message in Ghandi's philosophy, and in Michael Jackson's song. It is a simple one "if you want to see the world a better place, look in the mirror and make that change. It starts with YOU.

SURRENDER ALL — The Battle is NOT YOURS!!

*The Lord will Fight for you and You will
hold your PEACE; **Exodus 14:14***

*No matter what you
are going thru, remember that God only
wants a chance to use you
for the battle is not yours its the Lord's"*

In the approach to enter a softer more loving relationship with yourself, a key thing to remember is that while these steps are not rocket science, and on paper they don't look very complicated, in reality embracing these steps that translate in to learning to REALLY love yourself, can be challenging.

If you've been operating behind a Mask pretending to be something your not for any length of time, it may not be so easy to just wake up one morning and say "I'm going to stop pretending". If you've been resting in place, living in your mom's basement, staying on the same job and hating it, keeping at the same non-challenging work just going through the motion's when you know you can do better, stepping out may be overwhelming to you. And if you find yourself immersed in more than one of these steps to the Softer Side, and you may find it more and more difficult to see the value within you; then you need to tap into your power source.

If you find it turning into a daily battle to get over some past hurt or to stop being the one who creates the drama in yours and the lives of others; again you should know that by no means is it the expectation that these things can be executed without help. Especially the second step, moving away from the past so you can take a more effective step into the future. I realize that more often than not this looks good on paper, but in reality we are some times blocked – stuck if you will, in that past dark place. If we weren't, there really would be no issue.

You are NOT alone—aside from the fact that it is perfectly healthy, smart, and brave, to reach out for professional help; God is not blinded sided by our situations. He knows our weaknesses, and it is Him our creator, who is made stronger by our weakness.

Have you ever seen an announcement inside a box containing an appliance, a new TV, or piece of equipment that reads, "in case of malfunctioning, please return directly to the manufacturer". In our times of trouble or distress we get so caught up in trying to fix ourselves, or actually believing the seemingly hopelessness of our situation, that we forget did not make ourselves, and for the most part we don't have to fix ourselves. We should check with our manufacturer.

We all practice different faiths, celebrate spirituality and religion in various ways; it is equally as important to tap into our faith and spirituality when times are good in our lives, as it is in the times of our most distress. Whatever your belief system is, in time of challenge, frustration, grief, feelings of hopelessness and helplessness, this is the time to call upon it. You'll find it most encouraging when you stop and realize that in this great big universe, believing that there is something bigger than yourself can be a comfort. Just like finding the sign or notification on the appliance box we have received—we know that we don't have to struggle with the complexity of repairing this item or device on our own—we are limited in our skill and expertise—A manufacturer out there that we can turn it over to is indeed comforting.

Such is it with God our manufacturer he has a supply of replacement parts if we need them, he has the tools necessary to repair wounded spirits, broken hearts, damaged souls and a fractured mental well beings. And in the dark times we can take comfort in knowing this and reach out.

Conversely, there is nothing quite so hollow as counting on oneself to get through the valleys of life. Human failing will kick in and we'll find we are not connected to a power source—one that does not run out of steam. A Woman Entering a Softer More Loving Relationship with Herself recognizes that while in the natural she is 'good enough' just as she is, and her spiritual strength is based on a belief system that admits human failing. And she feels free to turn to God and say, "I'm stuck in this negative place, and I can't get out." (Psalm 138:3 "In the day when I cried out, You answered me, and made me bold with strength in my soul.")

One of the challenges women have in terms of surrendering and allowing for help to come into our lives, whether in the form of spirituality, professional help, or even friends; is sometimes the ego. Or in other words the "Super Woman" Syndrome. We erroneously believe that by seeking help or asking for help or admitting we need help, that we are being weak. Many times, however, it takes strength to get past ego, and pride, and fear, and admit that we are overwhelmed and need help.

Entering a Softer more Loving Relationship with ourselves is far more than just the rhetoric of just saying the words. It is taking deliberate action towards dealing with the issues in our lives that keep us from progressing. It is waking up to our condition and being happy with it, and making peace with it. Or it is waking up to our condition and, without beating ourselves up, saying I can be doing better, and subsequently exploring why we are not. It is examining ourselves to see what is holding us back and responding to the challenge of making the adjustments to go where we feel led.

We should know too that the same Manufacturer has also equipped us with the necessary tools to care for ourselves, and/or to recognize when we need to do some work—loving ourselves is reflected in our willingness to own our weaknesses and flaws, and to go to that place within that will provide us that "in your face" truth about ourselves.

This is the essence of what it is to LOVE WHO IT IS WE ARE—to respond to challenges, to recognize the pitfalls that keep us blocked in self pity, those feelings of anger and resentment of the past, and an unwillingness to take the responsibility for our own well being.

Until we take this journey, nothing will happen, we will stay trapped in those places where we blame others for every negative thing that happens to us. We will keep hiding behind drama that blocks the view and robs us of our productivity. This drama keeps us stuck in the past, wallowing around in self-pity, and/or self-recrimination for mis-deeds done to us, or for things we have not forgiven ourselves and staying on the edge of anger, so much so that we no longer recall what we were even angry about.

These are barriers to our positive outcomes in our lives that we could have. We can take control over these barriers,

by making the shift necessary to take our lives to the next level. This is the charge I leave with you today;

Avoid Hostile Confrontations
Make that Change
Spread your Wings
Drop the Drama
Leave the Baggage where you picked it up
Get over the Past
Take off the Mask

And be about the business of entering the destiny God has JUST FOR YOU

"ENTER A SOFTER MORE LOVING RELATIONSHIP WITH YOURSELF" --BECOME THE BEAUTIFUL, GIFTED, CREATIVE WOMAN GOD INTENDEND WHEN HE MADE YOU"

AFTER WORD

So it is finished, 13 years, 9 Woman to Woman empowerment symposiums, countless presentations to women and girls about rising out of their 'low self esteem", writing for groups of disenfranchised men and women and so much more.

Here is a volume that encompasses all of the conversations the women and I have had since 2003—which was years after my encounter with prophetess Mary Carter who prayed for me and spoke to me of the book that I should be writing or was about to write and would write.

My desire is that this information in this volume resonates within women; and drives home the message of self worth. I hope I have been able to do that.

There is one thing I know for sure and that is that the material within these pages comes from a place that had me all gnarled up on the inside for a long time.

The places were nestled so far down that I wasn't aware of them creating a myriad of problems for me. I had no clue that I was plagued with many of the issues I've written about in the book. However Softerside Seminars happened, in March of 2003—and by mid 2014 I was putting this volume together.

A few years after the encounter with prophetess Mary Carter, and after years of being asked repeatedly by one of my uncles "when was my book about him" going to be written. Ultimately, I just began following the invisible lead in the writing, and in the selection of topics.

I was following that lead up the roads and around the mazes; I slowly began to realize that what I was writing about – what I was telling women in my book, is what I should be doing myself.

As I wrote about being valued and valuing yourself, I knew that was speaking to me, As I wrote about recreating the way you see yourself and how important it was to honor, respect, love and celebrate the gifted beautiful woman God created when he made you, I begin feel funny because I wasn't doing these things myself. And though that was the very tag line I had been using over the past 13 years promoting Softer Side Seminars I no idea that I was NOT embracing what I was saying.

I was presenting "The 9 steps to the Softer Side—teaching, admonishing, laying out to women about moving out of angry places, getting over the past, avoiding drama, and more—it wasn't until I began putting the words I was speaking onto paper, that I came face to face with my TRUTH. The program I thought God put inside of me to give to other women was not so much for the "women" as it was intended for me. And it explains everything, prophetess Carter, my uncle, the nagging in my chest that stayed there long before I started Softer Side Seminars, and the fact that this book would not "quiet" itself within me. It was persistent in looking for me and It would not give up.

And I am glad… not just because of the discovering that the issues I believed were placed inside of me so I could help other women tackle were in reality MY ISSUES TOO.

I have also learned that this work in "becoming" all that God has destined us to become is not done in a 'minute', there is a lot of pushing and pulling in it." And we may not even get it right the first two or three times, but we must enter the process.

There is power that awaits us, there is wonder in the discovery….RENEE P. ALDRICH

"Leaving your Success to Chance, Minimizes
your chances of Succeeding.
Achieve your purpose on PURPOSE – Be Intentional"

Renee P. Aldrich